Selina Schuster

# White Beards of Power: A Comparison between Gandalf and Dumbledore

GRIN Verlag

**Bibliografische Information der Deutschen Nationalbibliothek:**

Die Deutsche Bibliothek verzeichnet diese Publikation in der Deutschen National-
bibliografie; detaillierte bibliografische Daten sind im Internet über http://dnb.d-
nb.de/ abrufbar.

**Imprint:**

Copyright © 2012 GRIN Verlag GmbH
Druck und Bindung: Books on Demand GmbH, Norderstedt Germany
ISBN: 978-3-656-57564-1

**This book at GRIN:**

http://www.grin.com/en/e-book/233126/white-beards-of-power-a-comparison-
between-gandalf-and-dumbledore

## GRIN - Your knowledge has value

Der GRIN Verlag publiziert seit 1998 wissenschaftliche Arbeiten von Studenten, Hochschullehrern und anderen Akademikern als eBook und gedrucktes Buch. Die Verlagswebsite www.grin.com ist die ideale Plattform zur Veröffentlichung von Hausarbeiten, Abschlussarbeiten, wissenschaftlichen Aufsätzen, Dissertationen und Fachbüchern.

## Visit us on the internet:

http://www.grin.com/

http://www.facebook.com/grincom

http://www.twitter.com/grin_com

**Name:** Selina Schuster

**Title:** Final Essay

# Long Beards of Power

All mighty wizards we encounter in literature usually possess one feature that immediately indicates their status as powerful sorcerers to the reader: a long, mostly white (occasionally grey) beard. A wizard simply can't be *that* powerful if he isn't depicted as an old man – very old to be precise – with a beard so enormous that he can effortlessly tuck its end into his belt. This cliché of the wise old man with magical abilities derives to a large extent from the depiction of Gandalf the Grey in J.R.R. Tolkien's fantasy novel *The Hobbit* and it's even more famous successor *The Lord of the Rings*. The character of Gandalf became not only the iconic prototype for the description of wizards in literature but it influenced a whole genre, making Gandalf the uber-father of all wizards, on whose typical features many authors still rely on. This also counts for the famous headmaster of a certain school for witchcraft and wizardry. Invented more than half a century after *The Hobbit*, J.K. Rowling's Albus Dumbledore from the *Harry Potter*-series heavily relies on the well-known image of how a versed magician has to act and look like. In fact he shares so many similarities with Gandalf that he could easily be mistaken for his a little less sarcastic younger brother. Not only do they share a striking resemblance concerning their outwards appearance, their temper and personality traits also resemble each other as well as their magical powers and their overall functions within the respective works they derive from.

The aspect which first comes to mind when one thinks about the two characters is their impressive and memorable appearance. Both are introduced right at the beginning of *The Hobbit* and *Harry Potter and the Philosopher's Stone* and get a very detailed description of their looks and attire. As the following citations show, long beards are obviously a serious must-have for wizards - may they reside in Middle Earth, Hogwarts or elsewhere: On the one hand we have Gandalf who is introduced as an 'old man with a staff. He had a tall pointed blue hat, a long grey cloak, a silver scarf over which his long white beard hung down below his waist, and immense black boots.' (Tolkien, 14) and on the other hand there is Dumbledore, who's 'tall, thin, and very old, judging by the silver of his hair and beard, which were both long enough to tuck them into his belt. He was wearing long robes, a purple cloak which swept over the ground and high-heeled, buckled boots.' (Rowling, 12). Their outward similarities strike the eye. In fact there exists such a strong resemblance between those two that at first glance one might think that it is one and the same person who is being described here. They look like the typical image of how a child would imagine a wizard. Tall, thin, if not haggard, wearing a particular style of clothing and as already mentioned a long beard that indicates they are actually very old and thus *very* powerful. And powerful they are indeed since both characters are described as highly capable wizards, right from the start. The first thing the reader actually gets to know about those two is that they are extraordinary men. They are highly experienced in many things, very clever, and world-wise. And apart from that they are – of course – very accomplished when it comes to the use of magic. In fact they are in all probability the most versed wizards to be found in their respective fictive worlds. Tolkien and Rowling draw the reader's attention to these special characteristics quite early in the stories. Although they don't let their magicians show off their enormous powers to demonstrate what they are capable of right away, they describe their respective wizards in such a fashion that it instantaneously becomes an established fact that these men are really important and mighty indeed. This happens even before the reader actually gets in touch with them since at the time of this character establishment they are both still rather dark horses who need and get an introduction so the reader can unmistakeably comprehend right from the beginning who and what they are. Tolkien introduces the character of Gandalf as follows: 'Gandalf! If you had heard only a quarter of what I have heard about him, and I have heard very little of all there is to hear, you would be prepared for any sort of remarkable tale. Tales and adventures sprouted up all over the place wherever he went, in the most extraordinary fashion' (Tolkien, 14). 'Gandalf, Gandalf! Not the wandering wizard who […] used to tell such wonderful tales at parties, about dragons and goblins and giants […]?' (Tolkien, 16). Right from the start the reader knows that there is something to Gandalf: He is as mysterious as he is famous and surely something extraordinary will happen as soon as this man shows up. J.K. Rowling takes this to an even higher level when it comes to the description of Dumbledore as a person, apart from his short first appearance in the first chapter: 'Albus Dumbledore, currently Headmaster of Hogwarts. Considered by many the greatest wizard of modern times, Professor Dumbledore is particularly famous for his defeat of the dark wizard Grindewald in 1945' (Rowling, 77). Both introductions contain basically the same content and serve the same purpose: The reader is ought to know that Gandalf and Dumbledore are great and well-known magicians.

Due to their established status as highly esteemed and powerful wizards who are hundreds of years more sophisticated and wiser than any other character in their respective stories, the functions they fulfil within them are also very much alike. In sum they can be called 'the guide' and 'the knight in shining armour'. They introduce the main characters to a new, unknown world and help them accustom to it during their journey. In Gandalf's case he is the one who draws the clueless little Hobbit Bilbo into an adventure the latter would have never dreamt of. Since he physically travels with him through Middle Earth, Gandalf on the one hand literally is the guide when it comes to the question which direction the party should go to and on the other he is the guide to this strange new world that opens itself right in front of Bilbo's eyes. Gandalf names and explains the creatures they encounter and the places they visit while he simultaneously appears as the knight in shining armour on several occasions in order to save the Hobbit and his company when they are in need. Furthermore, he gives background information to Bilbo and thus to the reader as well. In Dumbledore's case his function as a guide is a little more subdued. He does neither physically travel with Harry to Hogwarts nor does he show him around but nonetheless, he has always been a strong determinator in Harry's life since initially it was him who placed little Harry on his aunt's and uncle's doorstep and set the headstone for his 'first' life as a Muggle. When Harry finally comes to Hogwarts to enter his 'new life' as a wizard he supports him but keeps his actions hidden at first - for example he gives Harry the Invisibility Cloak for Christmas - before later on he definitely appears as a person Harry can rely on when he is in need of advice and help. Like Gandalf Dumbledore serves as a vehicle for background information e.g. when he explains to Harry how the Mirror of Erised works or how Harry was able to find the Philosopher's Stone. In both works it is clearly pointed out that the main characters rely very much on the wisdom, strength and support of the wizards as following citations show: 'go straight to the owlery and send Hedwig to Dumbledore. We need him.' (Rowling, 208). 'Now Gandalf too said farewell. Bilbo sat on the ground feeling very unhappy and wishing he was beside the wizard on his tall horse.' (Tolkien, 172). Although the main characters are capable of handling matters on their own - Harry is able to defend himself against Quirrell and Bilbo can save the dwarfs from being eaten alive by a horde of giant spiders - the first persons that come to the minds of the protagonists when things are starting to get dangerous are Gandalf and Dumbledore. And they actually *are* coming to the rescue: Even though Harry is able to stand his ground against Quirrell it eventually is Dumbledore who rushes to help just in time to defeat Quirrell/Voldemort thoroughly and saves Harry's life. And in *The Hobbit* it is Gandalf whose magic saves Bilbo and the dwarfs from being killed by an army of ogres. Once again the two wizards act very much alike and serve the same purpose throughout the progress of the novels. In sum it can be said that the similarities between Gandalf the Grey and Albus Dumbledore are really striking indeed.

Of course it can be argued about the exact extent of how much J.K. Rowling was influenced by the novel *The Hobbit* and its successor when it comes to the description of her own wizard and how much she modelled Albus Dumbledore after the character of Gandalf on purpose. But the more than obvious similarities suggest the assumption that J.K. Rowling was influenced by J.R.R. Tolkien's character – even if unconsciously. The reason for that might be that Gandalf became such an iconic prototype-figure for wizards that it influenced many works even decades after the creation of *The Hobbit*. The portrayal of mighty wizards as slightly eccentric old men with long white beards, pointy hats and a great portion of quirky humour became so well-recognized and generally accepted that it still is very present, not only in the heads of today's readers, but in the heads of contemporary authors as well. Bearing that and the very obvious points of resemblance between those two old men with the luxuriant crop of hair in mind, it is more than likely that this popular image inspired J.K. Rowling during the creational process of writing *Harry Potter and the Philosopher's Stone*.

## Works Cited

- Rowling, J.K. *Harry Potter and the Philosopher's Stone*. London: Bloomsberry, 2001. Print.
- Tolkien, J.R.R. *The Hobbit or There and Back Again*. London: Collins Modern Classics, 1998. Print.